The ABCs of

May You Always

Adventures, Blessings, Courage, and More

HAZELDEN

Keep Coming Back

CREATED BY MEIJI STEWART

ABC Writings © Meiji Stewart
Graphic Design & Illustration by Jeff Kahn
Graphic Production by Darryl Yee

The ABCs of May You Always Have...

ISBN 1-56838-745-8

Hazelden
P.O. Box 176
15251 Pleasant Valley Road
Center City, MN 55012-0176
1-800-328-9000
www.hazelden.org

05 04 03 02 01 6 5 4 3 2 1
ABC writings ©Meiji Stewart • Visit www.abcwritings.com

DEDICATED TO:

Marshall B. Rosenberg, the founder of the Center for Nonviolent Communication (CNVC) and to all those around the world who help share his message. Rosenberg's language of compassion has significantly improved the quality of my personal (especially with myself) and professional relationships. CNVC has also increased the clarity and consciousness with which I use language, and strengthened my intention to live a loving and compassionate life. Please visit *www.cnvc.org* for more information about his work.

THANKS TO:

Jeff Kahn for the great book cover and interior page designs. Please visit him at, *www.kahn-design.com* to see his wonderful designs and illustrations. Darryl Yee for his great production work and help with some of the interior illustrations. Neill Gibson, who is the passionate driving force behind PuddleDancer's promotion of Marshall Rosenberg's book *Nonviolent Communication*. Visit *www.nonviolentcommunication.com* for more information.

I also want to say thank you to my best friend and wife, Claudia, my daughter, Malia, my stepson, Tommy, my parents, Richard and Nannette, my sister, Leslie, my brothers, Ray and Scott, my nephews and nieces, Sebastien, Emilie, Skye, Luke, Jake, Jessie Nannette, Cairo, and Kamana, and to Richard, Jewels, Tom, Fumi, Jocelyne, and Stephen, and my father-in-law, Jim, and not forgetting, of course, our two greyhounds, Zoie and Sunset, and our two cats, Oliver and Tito.

May You Always Have...

Adventures to enrich your soul
Blessings showered upon you
Courage to be yourself
Dreams that come true
Enthusiasm to fuel your passions
Family, friends, and faith
Great things to look forward to
Health to live life to the fullest
Imagination to soar on
Joy to color your thoughts
Knowledge to empower you
Laughter to brighten your days
Memories to keep you warm

New horizons to explore
Opportunities to grow
Peace in your heart
Questions to ponder
Reverence for life
Strength to overcome
Time to say "I love you"
Understanding to care
Values to guide you
Wealth enough to share
Xuberance for your xistence
Youthfulness of spirit
Zest to make a difference

© Meiji Stewart

May you always have...

Adventures

to enrich your soul

Don't exclude yourself…
from precious moments
warm encounters
beautiful attitudes
majestic discoveries
flowing intimacies
sensory development
for these are the jewels placed
in the crown of your destiny.

~Walter Rinder

Adventure is worthwhile in itself.

~Amelia Earhart

*Twenty years from now you will be more disappointed by
the things that you didn't do than by the things you did.
So throw off the bowlines. Sail away from the safe harbor.
Catch the trade winds in your sail. Explore. Dream. Discover.*

~Mark Twain

My favorite thing is to go where I've never been.

~Diane Arbus

One way to get the most out of life is to look upon it as an adventure.

~William Feather

Adventure is not outside a man; it is within.

~David Grayson

Grand adventures await those who are willing to turn the corner.

~Fortune cookie

If you approach each new person you meet in a spirit of adventure, you will find yourself endlessly fascinated by new channels of thought and experience and personality that you encounter.

~Eleanor Roosevelt

Security is mostly a superstition. It does not exist in nature. Life is either a daring adventure or nothing.

~Helen Keller

*A*bove all, challenge yourself.
You may well surprise yourself at what strengths you have,
what you can accomplish.

~Cecile M. Springer

*M*an cannot discover new oceans until he has
courage to lose sight of the shore.

~Author unknown

*M*ake voyages. Attempt them. There's nothing else.

~Tennessee Williams

May you always have...

Blessings

showered upon you

Give thanks for unknown blessings already on their way.

~Native American saying

Learn to get in touch with silence within yourself and know that everything in this life has a purpose. There are no mistakes, no coincidences, all events are blessings given to us to learn from.

~Elisabeth Kübler-Ross

Just to be is a blessing. Just to live is holy.

~Abraham Heschel

God bless all those that I love;
God bless all those that love me;
God bless all those that love those that I love
and all those that love those that love me.

~Author unknown

Everything that happens to you is your teacher.
The secret is to learn to sit at the feet of your own life and be taught
by it. Everything that happens is either a blessing which is also a
lesson, or a lesson which is also a blessing.

~Polly Berrien Berends

Reflect upon your present blessings, of which every man has many;
not on your past misfortunes, of which all men have some.

~Charles Dickens

*May God's richest blessing be upon you today
and throughout the year—and may those blessings
flow through you to touch the lives of everyone you meet.*

~Gary Smalley

*In reality, serendipity accounts for 1 percent of the
blessings we receive in life, work, and love.
The other 99 percent is due to our efforts.*

~Peter McWilliams

*T*he golden opportunity you are seeking is in yourself.
It is not in your environment; it is not in luck or chance,
or the help of others; it is in yourself alone.

~Orison Swett Marden

*M*ay you live as long as you want to.
May you want to as long as you live.

~Old English toast

May you always have...

Courage

to be yourself

Υou have a unique message to deliver, a unique song to sing,
a unique act of love to bestow. This message, this song, and this act
of love have been entrusted exclusively to the one and only you.

~John Powell

$\mathcal{I}$f you ask me what I came into the world to do, I will tell you:
I came to live out loud.

~Émile Zola

*Everyone has talent. What is rare is the courage
to follow the talent to the dark place where it leads.*

~Erica Jong

*Cultivate your garden. Do not depend upon teachers to educate
you....Follow your own bent, pursue your curiosity bravely, express
yourself, make your own harmony.*

~Will Durant

Your work is to discover your world and then with all your heart give yourself to it.

~Buddha

Courage and perseverance have a magical talisman, before which difficulties disappear and obstacles vanish into air.

~John Quincy Adams

*One doesn't discover new lands without consenting
to lose sight of the shore for a very long time.*

~André Gide

*Courage doesn't always roar. Sometimes courage is the little
voice at the end of the day that says, "I'll try again tomorrow."*

~Mary Anne Radmacher-Hershey

Every one of us has in him a continent of undiscovered character.
Blessed is he who acts the Columbus to his own soul.

~Author unknown

Before his death, Rabbi Zyusa said,
"In the coming world, they will not ask me:
'Why were you not Moses?' They will ask me:
'Why were you not Zyusa?'"

~Martin Buber

May you always have...

Dreams

that come true

Are you in earnest? Then seize this very minute. What you can do, or dream you can, begin it; Boldness has genius, power and magic in it; only engage and then the mind grows heated; Begin, and then the work will be completed.

~Johann Wolfgang von Goethe

We all have possibilities we don't know about. We can do things we don't even dream we can do.

~Dale Carnegie

If one advances confidently in the direction of his dreams, and endeavors to live the life he imagined, he will meet with a success unexpected in common hours.

~Henry David Thoreau

Keep a daily diary of your dreams, goals and accomplishments. If your life is worth living, it's worth recording.

~Marilyn Grey

Always keep one still,
secret spot where dreams may go and,
sheltered so, may thrive and grow.

~Louise Priscott

Commitment is the willingness to do whatever it takes to get
what you want. A true commitment is a heartfelt promise to
yourself from which you will not back down. Many people have
dreams and many have good intentions but few are willing to
make the commitment for their attainment.

~David McNally

*I have a dream my four little children
will one day live in a nation where they
will not be judged by the color of their skin
but by content of their character.*

~Martin Luther King Jr.

*The future belongs to those who believe in the
beauty of their dreams.*

~Eleanor Roosevelt

There are people who put their dreams in a little box and say, "Yes, I've got dreams, of course, I've got dreams." Then they put the box away and bring it out once in a while to look in it, and yep, they're still there. These are great dreams, but they never even get out of the box. It takes an uncommon amount of guts to put your dreams on the line, to hold them up and say, "How good or bad am I?" That's where the courage comes in.

~Erma Bombeck

Nothing is impossible; there are ways that lead to everything.

~François de la Rochefoucauld

26

May you always have...

Enthusiasm

to fuel your passions

How we live, how we feel, what we think and what we become all
depend on personal decisions. You are the master of your life.
You can choose to celebrate life, live fully and live healthfully.
Health is a choice! Happiness is a choice! Peace is a choice!
And enthusiasm is the elixir that generates change,
nourishes the body and feeds the soul.

~Susan Smith Jones

Wake up with a smile and go after life.
Live it, enjoy it, taste it, smell it, feel it.

~Joe Knapp

We either make ourselves happy or miserable.
The amount of work is the same.

~Carlos Castaneda

Passion is not necessarily something we have,
it's something we choose.

~Susan Carlson

We act as though comfort and luxury
were the chief requirements of life,
when all that we need to make us really happy
is something to be enthusiastic about.

~Charles Kingsley

This is a record of your time. This is your movie.
Live out your dreams and fantasies.
Whisper questions to the sphinx at night.
Sit for hours at sidewalk cafes and drink with your heroes.
Make pilgrimages to Mougins and Abiquiu. Look up and down.
Believe in the unknown for it is there. Live in many places. Live with
flowers and music. Keep a record of your time. Learn to read well.
Learn to listen and speak well. Know your country, know your world,
know your history, know yourself. Take care of yourself physically and
mentally. You owe it to yourself. Be good to those around you.
And do all of these things with passion. Give all that you can.
Remember, Life is short and Death is long.

~Fritz Shoulder

*The moment you commit and quit holding back,
all sorts of unforseen incidents, meetings and material assistance
will rise up to help you. The simple act of commitment
is a powerful magnet for help.*

~Napolean Hill

Nothing is interesting if you're not interested.

~Helen MacInness

*You cannot kindle a fire in any other
heart until it is burning in your own.*

~Ben Sweetland

*The more passions and desires one has,
the more ways one has of being happy.*

~Charlotte Catherine

*Let enthusiasm radiate in your voice, your actions,
your facial expressions, your personality, the words you use,
and the thoughts you think!*

~Ralph Waldo Emerson

May you always have...

Family,
friends, and faith

*When Mother Teresa received her Nobel prize,
she was asked, "What can we do to promote world peace?"
She replied, "Go home and love your family."*

~Mother Teresa

*We are each of us angels with only one wing.
And we can fly only by embracing each other.*

~Luciano de Crescenzo

The ABCs of Loving Families...

Accentuate the positive.

Balance work, rest, and play.

Communicate with mutual respect.

Don't sweat the small stuff.

Encourage healthy habits.

Find ways to say "I love you."

Grow self-esteem and self-acceptance.

Help each other do for themselves.

Inspire individuality and interdependence.

Juggle schedules to be there.

Know there are no perfect families.

Look for the best in each other.

Make the world a better place.

Nurture abilities and talents.

Openly talk about whatever's up.

Provide safety and security.

Quickly mend fences and move on.

Remind yourself of your uniqueness.

Savor memories and traditions.

Take time to really listen and care.

Understand how precious family time is.

Value presence more than presents.

Work things out compassionately.

Xperience life's ups and downs together.

Yearn to bequeath a spirit of reverence.

Zest to create a happy home.

Each friend represents a world in us, a world possibly not born until they arrive, and it is only in this meeting that a new world is born.

~Anaïs Nin

*Do not save your loving speeches
for your friends till they are dead;
Do not write them on their tombstones,
speak them rather now instead.*

~Anna Cummins

Faith is an oasis in the heart which will never be reached by the caravan of thinking.

~Kahlil Gibran

There is a reason for all things. Faith means we don't always have to have the answer.

~Petey Parker

Faith is not shelter against difficulties but belief in the face of all contradictions.

~Paul Tournier

I'm so glad you are here....
It helps me to realize how beautiful my world is.

~Rainer Maria Rilke

There is no wilderness like a life without friends;
friendship multiplies blessings and minimizes misfortunes;
it is a unique remedy against adversity, and it soothes the soul.

~Baltasar Gracian

I always prefer to believe the best of everybody—
it saves so much trouble.

~Rudyard Kipling

May you always have...

Great things

to look forward to

The best things in life aren't things.

~Art Buchwald

*The great thing in this world is not so much where we are,
but in what direction we are moving.*

~Oliver Wendell Holmes

*The purpose of life is to matter, to count, to stand for something,
to have it make some difference that we have lived at all.*

~Leo Buscaglia

Life's a pretty precious and wonderful thing.
You can't sit down and let it lap around you....
You have to plunge into it; you have to dive through it!
And you can't save it; you can't store it up;
you can't hoard it in a vault. You've got to taste it;
you've got to use it. The more you use, the more you have....
That's the miracle of it!

~Kyle Chrichton

Be thou the rainbow to the storms of life!

~George Gordon Byron

May you always have...Great things to look forward to

Υou are the one person for whom you are entirely responsible.
Your world, your life can be better only if you make it so.
As you improve yourself, you influence all others around you.
Keep in mind that you came into this life with a purpose to perform.

~Harold Sherman

$\mathcal{D}$estiny is not a matter of chance, it is a matter of choice.
It is not a thing to be waited for; it is a thing to be achieved.

~William Jennings Bryan

To change one's life: Start immediately.
Do it flamboyantly. No exceptions.

~William James

The realization of the self is only possible
if one is productive, if one can give birth
to one's own potentialities.

~Johann Wolfgang von Goethe

There is a universal truth that I have found in my work. Everybody longs to be loved. And the greatest thing we can do is let somebody know that they are loved and capable of loving.

~Fred Rogers

The greatest thing is, at any moment, to be willing to give up who we are in order to become all that we can become.

~Max De Pree

May you always have...

Health

to live life to the fullest

Health necessarily involves the coordination and congruence of all aspects of one's being, including communications and relationships with others and with the environment. It embraces every aspect of life, including diet, exercise, work, play and relaxation.

~Emmett E. Miller

The biggest disease today is not leprosy or tuberculosis, but rather the feeling of being unwanted.

~Mother Teresa

Any healthy man can go without food for two days—but not without poetry.

~Charles-Pierre Baudelaire

Everything you eat affects you profoundly.

~Chinese proverb

I believe that staying deeply connected with the divine energy within us helps free us "from age-old theology and notions of people being sinners deserving of punishment and reward." When we look behind these moralistic judgments that we make of ourselves, and others, and see only the needs that aren't being met, we no longer feel anger, depression, guilt and shame.

~Marshall B. Rosenberg

*H*appiness is good health and a bad memory.

~Ingrid Bergman

*Use your health, even to the point of wearing it out.
That is what it is for.
Spend all you have before you die; do not outlive yourself.*

~George Bernard Shaw

*You must live in the present, launch yourself on every
wave, find your eternity in each moment. Fools stand on
their island opportunities and look toward another land.
There is no other land, there is no other life but this,
or the like of this.*

~Henry David Thoreau

Don't smoke too much, drink too much, eat too much or work too much. We're all on the road to the grave— but there's no reason to be in the passing lane.

~Robert Orben

To your good health, old friend, may you live for a thousand years, and I be there to count them.

~Robert Smith Surtees

May you always have...

Imagination

to soar on

All the resources we need are in the mind.

~Theodore Roosevelt Jr.

*Every candle ever lit; every home,
bridge, cathedral or city ever built;
every act of human kindness, discovery,
daring, artistry or advancement started
first in someone's imagination,
and then worked its way out.*

~Gil Atkinson

The ABCs of Creativity...

Awakening your genius.

Being alive in the moment.

Cultivating change and curiosity.

Dreaming, dabbling, and daring.

Exploring infinite possibilities.

Fostering "trains of thought."

Going back to the drawing board.

Hard work and having fun too.

Indulging in your potential.

Joyful intensity and wild abandon.

Kindling your uniqueness.

Letting go of inhibitions.

Mindfulness and magic.

Never giving up on your dreams.

On- and off-the-wall thinking.

Playing, prospecting, and perusing.

Questioning and brainstorming.

Reading between the lines.

Soaring on your imagination.

Transcending the traditional.

Using all of your senses.

Visualizing the impossible.

Wallowing in wonder.

Xperiencing paradigm shifts.

Yearning for intuitive guidance.

Zestful zigzagging and zanyness.

©Meiji Stewart

It is with the heart that one sees rightly;
what is essential is invisible to the eye.

~Antoine de Saint-Exupéry

It's not what you look at that matters, it's what you see.

~Henry David Thoreau

Imagination is the beginning of creation.
We imagine what we desire;
we will what we imagine;
and at last we create what we will.

~George Bernard Shaw

You are the product of your own brainstorm.

~Rosemary Konner Steinbaum

*M*aybe we should develop a Crayola bomb as our next secret weapon. A happiness weapon. A beauty bomb. And every time a crisis developed, we would launch one. It would explode high in the air—explode softly—and send thousands, millions, of little parachutes into the air. Floating down to earth—boxes of Crayolas. And we wouldn't go cheap, either—not little boxes of eight. Boxes of sixty-four, with the sharpener built right in. With silver and gold and copper, magenta and peach and lime, amber and umber and all the rest. And people would smile and get a little funny look on their faces and cover the world with imagination.

~Robert Fulghum

May you always have...

Joy

to color your thoughts

It is a fine seasoning for joy to think of those we love.

~Jean-Baptiste Molière

Joy is not in things, it is in us.

~Richard Wagner

The more passionately we love life,
the more intensely we experience the joy of life.

~Jurgen Moltman

When we give from the heart, we do so out of a joy that springs forth whenever we willingly enrich another person's life. This kind of giving benefits both the giver and the receiver. The receiver enjoys the gift without worrying about the consequences that accompany gifts given out of fear, guilt, shame, or desire for gain. The giver benefits from the enhanced self-esteem that results when we see our efforts contributing to someone's well-being.

~Marshall B. Rosenberg

This is the true joy in life; being used for a purpose recognized by yourself as a mighty one.

~George Bernard Shaw

There is nothing more beautiful than a rainbow, but it takes both rain and sunshine to make a rainbow. If life is to be rounded and many-colored like the rainbow, both joy and sorrow must come to it.

~Author unknown

Imagine the joy of day by day growing into a fuller understanding of who you are—who you are, really, the power you really have.

~Tae Yun Kim

Your success and happiness lie in you.
External conditions are the accidents of life.
The great enduring realities are love and service.
Joy is the holy fire that keeps our purpose warm
and our intelligence aglow.
Resolve to keep happy, and your joy and you
shall form an invincible host against difficulty.

~Helen Keller

All the world is searching for joy and happiness, but these cannot be purchased for any price in any marketplace, because they are virtues that come from within, and like rare jewels must be polished, for they shine brightest in the light of faith, and in the services of brotherly love.

~Lucille R. Taylor

There are joys which long to be ours. God sends ten thousand truths, which come about us like birds seeking inlet; but we are shut up to them, and so they bring us nothing, but sit and sing awhile upon the roof, and then fly away.

~Henry Ward Beecher

May you always have...

Knowledge

to empower you

I have learned silence from the talkative,
tolerance from the intolerant,
and kindness from the unkind.
I should not be ungrateful to those teachers.

~Kahlil Gibran

I have never let my schooling interfere with my education.

~Mark Twain

The longer the island of knowledge,
the longer the shore line of wonder.

~Ralph W. Sockman

A man who does not read good books
has no advantage over the man who can't read them.

~Mark Twain

It is what we think we know already that
often prevents us from learning.

~Claude Bernard

Two important things are to have a genuine interest in people and to be kind to them. Kindness, I've discovered, is everything in life.

~Isaac Bashevis Singer

Punishment damages goodwill and self-esteem, and shifts our attention from the intrinsic value of an action to external consequences. Blaming and punishing fail to contribute to the motivations we would like to inspire in others.

~Marshall B. Rosenberg

*The shoe that fits one person pinches another;
there is no recipe for living that suits all cases.*

~Carl Gustav Jung

*No man ever will unfold the capacities of his own intellect
who does not at least checker his own life with solitude.*

~Thomas De Quincey

What sculpture is to a block of marble, education is to the soul.

~Joseph Addison

Knowledge is power, but enthusiasm pulls the switch.

~Ivern Ball

Action is the proper fruit of knowledge.

~Thomas Fuller

May you always have...

Laughter

to brighten your days

The first thing to be done is laughter, because that sets the trend for the whole day. If you wake up laughing, you will soon begin to feel how absurd life is. Nothing is serious: even your disappointments are laughable; even your pain is laughable; even you are laughable.

~Osho

Those who bring sunshine to the lives of others cannot keep it from themselves.

~J. M. Barrie

It is bad to suppress laughter.
It goes back down and spreads to your hips.

~Steve Allen

For me, a hearty "belly laugh" is one of the beautiful
sounds in the world.

~Bennett Cerf

Outside of a dog, a book is man's best friend.
Inside of a dog, it's too dark to read.

~Groucho Marx

The ABCs of Happiness...

Adventures in self-discovery.

Being true to yourself.

Creating a life you love.

Disposition, not circumstance.

Enjoying what you have.

Finding balance.

Growing friendships.

Having someone to love.

an Inside job, go within.

a Journey of the heart.

Knowing when to let go.

Learning from your mistakes.

Making the best of any situation.

Not taking things personally.

are Optional, so is misery.

Progress, not perfection.

the Quality of your thoughts.

Reverence for body, mind, and spirit.

Spending time with loved ones.

Today well lived.

Understanding more, judging less.

Valuing feelings and needs.

Whatever makes your heart sing.

Xpressing your truth lovingly.

Your choice, if not now, when?

Zzzzzzz's, a good night's sleep.

Don't evaluate your life in terms of achievements...
Instead, wake up and appreciate everything you encounter
along your path. Enjoy the flowers that are there for your
pleasure. Tune in to the sunrise, the little children,
the laughter, the rain, and the birds. Drink it all in....
There is no way to happiness; happiness is the way.

~Wayne W. Dyer

By being frequently in the company of children,
we may learn to recapture the will to laugh and
the art of laughing at will.

~Julius Gordon

To laugh often and much; to win the respect of intelligent people and the affection of children; to earn the appreciation of honest critics and endure the betrayal of false friends; to appreciate beauty; to find the best in others; to leave the world a bit better, whether by a healthy child, a garden patch or a redeemed social condition; to know even one life has breathed easier because you have lived. This is to have succeeded.

~Ralph Waldo Emerson

The human race has one really effective weapon, and that is laughter.

~Mark Twain

May you always have...

to keep you warm

People must learn to gather adventures and experiences rather than things or possessions. Possessions will burden you, but adventures are memories which will enrich your soul and they will last forever.

~Alfred A. Montapert

Keep a diary or daily win book to record your aspirations and accomplishments. If your life is worth living, it's worth recording.

~Oliver Wendell Holmes

*I wish I would have put as much emotion into my relationships
with my mom and dad as I do now in my memories of them.
We should pay more attention when we are making our memories.
If we did, we wouldn't have so many regrets
when all we have are memories.*

~Author unknown

*Memory is like a child walking along a seashore.
You never can tell what small pebble it will pick up
and store away among its treasured things.*

~Pierce Harris

Kind words are jewels that live in the heart and soul and remain as blessed memories years after they have been spoken.

~Marvea Johnson

You never know when you're making a memory.

~Rickie Lee Jones

God gave us memory so that we might have roses in December.

~J. M. Barrie

Memories, important yesterdays, were once today's.
Treasure and notice today.

~Gloria Gaither

Cherish all your happy moments:
they make a fine cushion for old age.

~Booth Tarkington

If you tell the truth, you don't have to remember anything.

~Mark Twain

We didn't know that morning,
God was going to call your name.
In life we loved you dearly,
In death we do the same.
It broke our hearts to lose you,
You did not go alone,
For part of us went with you,
The day God called you home.
You left us beautiful memories,
Your love is still our guide,
And though we cannot see you,
You are always by our side.
Our family chain is broken,
And nothing seems the same,
But as God calls us one by one,
The chain will link again.

~Author unknown

May you always have...

New horizons
to explore

*Our task is to explore, to celebrate and delight
in the depths of the universe.*

~Brian Swimme

*You must learn day by day, year by year, to broaden your horizon.
The more things you love, the more you are interested in,
the more you enjoy, the more you are indignant about,
the more you have left when anything happens.*

~Ethel Barrymore

You will never "find" time for anything.
If you want time you must make it.

~Charles Buxton

It is more important to know where you are going than
to get there quickly. Do not mistake action for achievement.

~Mabel Newcomer

There are many wonderful things that will never be done
if you do not do them.

~Charles D. Gill

*O*ne of the most tragic things I know about human nature is that all of us tend to put off living. We are all dreaming of some magical rose garden over the horizon—instead of enjoying the roses that are blooming outside our windows today.

~Dale Carnegie

*Y*ou are the only one who can stretch your own horizon.

~Edgar F. Magnin

*The real voyage of discovery consists not in seeking
new landscapes but in having new eyes.*

~Marcel Proust

*The world is round and the place which may seem
like the end may also be only the beginning.*

~Ivy Baker Priest

Most of the things worth doing in the world had been declared impossible before they were done.

~Louis D. Brandeis

You may be disappointed if you fail, but you are doomed if you don't try.

~Beverly Sills

The Wright brothers flew right through the smoke screen of impossibility.

~Charles Kettering

May you always have...

Opportunities

to grow

Why stay we on the earth except to grow?

~Robert Browning

Life's challenges are not supposed to paralyze you, they're supposed to help you discover who you are.

~Bernice Johnson Reagon

To be what we are, and to become what we are capable of becoming, is the only end of life.

~Robert Louis Stevenson

The chief danger in life is that you may take too many precautions.

~Alfred Adler

Progress always involves risks.
You can't steal second base and keep your foot on first.

~Frederick B. Wilcox

I am always doing that which I cannot do,
in order that I may learn how to do it.

~Pablo Picasso

The ABCs of Dare To...

Ask for what you want.

Believe in yourself.

Change your mind.

Do what you love.

Enjoy each and every day.

Follow your heart's desire.

Give more than you receive.

Have a sense of humor.

Insist on being yourself.

Join in more.

Kiss and make up.

Love and be loved.

Make new friends.

Nurture your spirit.

Overcome adversity.

Play more.

Question conformity.

Reach for the stars.

Speak your truth.

Take personal responsibility.

Understand more, judge less.

Volunteer your time.

Walk through fear.

Xperience the moment.

Yearn for grace.

be Zany.

©*Meiji Stewart*

When one door closes another opens. Expect that new door to reveal even greater wonders and glories and surprises. Feel your self grow with every experience. And look for the reason for it.

~Eileen Caddy

Life does not accommodate you, it shatters you.
It is meant to and couldn't do it better.
Every seed destroys its container or else
there would be no growth, no fruition.

~Florida Scott Maxwell

*Unless you try to do something
beyond what you have already mastered, you will never grow.*

~Ronald E. Osborn

Our main task is to give birth to ourselves.

~Erich Fromm

*We must always change, renew, rejuvenate ourselves;
otherwise we harden.*

~Johann Wolfgang von Goethe

May you always have...

Peace

in your heart

May Your World Be Full of Peas

Give Peas a Chance

©*Meiji Stewart/Jeff Kahn*

May you have warmth in your igloo,
oil in your lamp, and peace in your heart.

~Inuit saying

My religion is very simple. My religion is kindness.

~Dalai Lama

If we have no peace, it is because
we have forgotten that we belong to each other.

~Mother Teresa

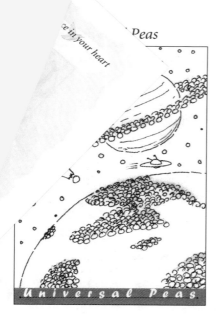

...e in your heart

...Peas

Universal Peas

Peas on Earth

Peas on Earth

©Meiji Stewart/Jeff Kahn

There is no need to go to India or anywhere else to find peace. You will find that deep place of silence right in your room, your garden or even your bathtub.

~Elisabeth Kübler-Ross

The best and most beautiful things in the world cannot be seen or even touched. They must be felt with the heart.

~Helen Keller

Visualize World Peas

May Your Heart Be Full of Peas

May you always have...

Questions?

to ponder

What happens to disconnect us from our compassionate nature, leading us to behave violently and exploitatively? And conversely, what allows some people to stay connected to their compassionate nature under even the most trying circumstances?

~Marshall B. Rosenberg

We are what we think.
All that we are arises with our thoughts.
With our thoughts, we make our world.

~Buddha

O*n a garden wall in Peking, China,*
was a brass plate about two feet long with these words:
Enjoy yourself. It is later than you think!
Well, maybe it is later than you think;
why don't you do something about it?

~Charles W. Miller

I*f you were going to die soon and had only*
one phone call you could make, who would you call
and what would you say? And why are you waiting?

~Stephen Levine

It is not enough to be busy....The question is: What are we busy about ?

~Henry David Thoreau

If there were dreams to sell, what would you buy?

~Thomas Lovell Beddoes

What would you attempt to do if you knew you could not fail?

~Author unknown

What do you want to do? What do you want to be?
What do you want to have? Where do you want to go?
Who do you want to go with? How do you plan to get there?
Write it down. Go do it. Enjoy it. Share it.
It doesn't get much simpler or better than that.

~Lee Iacocca

If you do not get it from yourself, where will you go for it?

~ Buddha

*W*as she so loved because her eyes were so beautiful
or were her eyes so beautiful because she was so loved?

~Anzia Yezierska

*W*hat appreciation might someone give you that
would leave you jumping for joy?

~Marshall B. Rosenberg

May you always have...

Reverence *for life*

The more you become a connoisseur of gratitude,
the less you are a victim of resentment, depression,
and despair. Gratitude will act as an elixir that will
gradually dissolve the hard shell of your ego—your
need to possess and control—and transform you into
a generous being. The sense of gratitude produces
true spiritual alchemy, makes us magnanimous—
large souled.

~Sam Keen

*Sit in reverie, and watch the changing color of the waves
that break upon the idle seashore of the mind.*

~Henry Wadsworth Longfellow

*By having reverence for life,
we enter into a spiritual relation with the world.*

~Albert Schweitzer

The Zen master Ling Chi said that the miracle is not to walk on burning charcoal or in the thin air or on the water; the miracle is just to walk on earth. You breathe in. You become aware of the fact that you are alive. You are still alive and you are walking on this beautiful planet.... The greatest of all miracles is to be alive.

~Thich Nhat Hanh

I love to think of nature as an unlimited broadcasting station through which God speaks to us every hour, if only we will tune in.

~George Washington Carver

When you come right down to it,
the secret of having it all is loving it all.

~Joyce Brothers

That it will never come again is
what makes life so sweet.

~Emily Dickinson

God gave you a gift of 86,400 seconds today.
Have you used one to say "thank you"?

~William A. Ward

*Expect the best. Convert problems into opportunities.
Be dissatisfied with the status quo. Focus on where you want to
go, instead of where you're coming from. Decide to be happy,
knowing it's an attitude, a habit gained from daily practice,
and not a result or payoff.*

~Dennis Waitley

*The invariable mark of wisdom is to see
the miraculous in the common.*

~Ralph Waldo Emerson

May you always have...

Strength

to overcome

Nothing in the world can take the place of persistence. Talent will not; nothing is more common than unsuccessful men with talent. Genius will not; unrewarded genius is almost a proverb. Education will not; the world is full of educated failures. Persistence and determination alone are omnipotent.

~Calvin Coolidge

Strength does not come from physical capacity. It comes from an indomitable will.

~Mohandas Gandhi

The ABCs of Don't Quit...

Anything can happen.

Bend, don't break.

Challenge your potential.

Destiny is a choice.

Effort creates opportunities.

Fly in the face of adversity.

Get back up and try again.

Hold on to your vision.

Impress yourself.

Just dig a little deeper.

Keep knocking on doors.

Learn from mistakes.

Motivate with compassion.

Nothing worthwhile comes easy.

Own a positive attitude.

Problems hold messages.

Question what's not working.

Regroup when you need to.

Shoot for the moon.

Think outside the box.

Understand "this too shall pass."

Value knowing when to walk away.

Work smarter not harder.

Xhaust all possibilities.

You can if you think you can.

Zest to do your best.

©*Meiji Stewart*

The people who get on in this world are the people who get up and look for the circumstances they want, and if they can't find them, make them.

~George Bernard Shaw

Did you ever hear of a man who had striven all his life faithfully and singly toward an object, and in no measure obtained it? If a man constantly aspires, is he not elevated?

~Henry David Thoreau

It is for us to make the effort. The result is always in God's hands.

~Mohandas Gandhi

If your determination is fixed, I do not counsel you to despair.
Few things are impossible to diligence and skill.
Great works are performed not by strength but perseverance.

~Samuel Johnson

I won't have any money to leave behind.
I won't have the fine and luxurious things of life to leave behind.
But I just want to leave a committed life behind.

~Martin Luther King Jr.

Always bear in mind that your own resolution to succeed
is more important than any other one thing.

~Abraham Lincoln

May you always have...

Time

to say "I love you"

Love is not something you feel. It is something you do.

~David Wilkerson

Don't say you don't have enough time. You have exactly the same number of hours per day that were given to Pasteur, Michelangelo, Mother Teresa, Helen Keller, Leonardo da Vinci, Thomas Jefferson, and Albert Einstein.

~H. Jackson Brown Jr.

*I*f we all discovered that we had only five minutes left to say all that we wanted to say, every telephone booth would be occupied by people calling other people to tell them that they loved them.

~Christopher Morley

*T*oday say "I love you" to those you love.
The eternal silence is long enough to be silent in,
and that awaits us all.

~George Eliot

*Love doesn't make the world go 'round.
Love is what makes the ride worthwhile.*

~Franklin P. Jones

*The happiness of life is made up of minute fractions—the little
soon forgotten charities of a kiss or smile, a kind look,
a heartfelt compliment, and the countless infinitesimals of
pleasurable and genial feeling.*

~Samuel Taylor Coleridge

The ABCs of Love...

e Answer, whatever the question.

Being there to wipe away the tears.

Choice, color the world beautiful.

Doing, actions speak louder than words.

Everywhere, if you look for it.

Forgiving, and for giving.

Gratitude for all that is, was, and will be.

Holding hands more, hurrying less.

Inclusive, not exclusive.

Journeying together on our own paths.

Kindness, do what you can when you can.

Laughing, listening, and letting go.

Magical, the more you give, the more you receive.

Now, why wait until tomorrow?

Open-minded, there are many sides to every story.

Powerful, be the cause of wonderful things.

Quick to build bridges and take down walls.

Realizing, you wouldn't want it any other way.

Sharing, dare to care.

Thoughtful, tender, and true.

Unconditional, no ifs, ands, or buts.

Vital, like sunshine and rain to a flower.

Willingness to see through the eyes of a child.

Xpressing your truth, knowing the answers will come.

Yearning for connection, not correction.

Zany, dive deep into the mystery.

©Meiji Stewart

Do not keep the alabaster boxes of your love and tenderness
sealed up until your friends are dead. Fill their lives with
sweetness. Speak approving, cheering words while their ears
can hear them and while their hearts can be thrilled by them.

~Henry Ward Beecher

May you always have...

Understanding

to care

*It is understanding that gives us an ability to have peace.
When we understand the other fellow's viewpoint,
and he understands ours, then we can sit down
and work out our differences.*

~Harry S. Truman

*If I had known what trouble you were bearing;
what griefs were in the silence of your face;
I would have been more gentle, and more caring,
and tried to give you gladness for a space.*

~Mary Carolyn Davies

Words are windows, or they're walls,
They sentence us, or set us free.
If I seemed to put you down,
If you felt I didn't care,
Try to listen through my words
To the feelings that we share.

~Ruth Bebermeyer

Behind intimidating messages are simply people
appealing to us to meet their needs.

~Marshall B. Rosenberg

You must understand the whole of life, not just one little part of it. That is why you must read, that is why you must look at the skies, that is why you must sing and dance, and write poems, and suffer, and understand, for all that is life.

~J . Krishnamurti

Could a greater miracle take place than for us to look through each other's eys for an instant?

~Henry David Thoreau

When you understand, you cannot help but love.
You cannot get angry. To develop understanding,
you have to practice looking at all living beings with
the eyes of compassion. When you understand, you love.
And when you love, you naturally act in a way that
can relieve the suffering of people.

~Thich Nhat Hanh

Knowing what to say is not always necessary;
just the presence of a caring friend can make a world of difference.

~Sheri Curry

*The motto should not be, "Forgive one another."
Rather, "Understand one another."*

~Emma Goldman

*We cannot change anything until we accept it.
Condemnation does not liberate, it oppresses.*

~Carl Gustav Jung

May you always have...

Values

to guide you

Sow a thought and you reap an act;
Sow an act and you reap a habit;
Sow a habit and you reap a character;
Sow a character and you reap a destiny.

~Samuel Smiles

I care not what others think of what I do,
but I care very much about
what I think of what I do. That is character!

~Theodore Roosevelt

*Happiness is that state of consciousness
which proceeds from the achievement of one's values.*

~Ayn Rand

*What lies behind us and what lies before us are tiny matters,
compared to what lies within us.*

~Ralph Waldo Emerson

Be not simply good; be good for something.

~Henry David Thoreau

Integrity is what we do, what we say, and what we say we do.

~Don Galer

I conceive that the great part of the miseries of mankind are brought upon them by false estimates they have made of the value of things.

~Benjamin Franklin

The most important thing in the world is that you make yourself the greatest, grandest, most wonderful loving person in the world because this is what you are going to be giving to your children—to all those you meet.

~Leo Buscaglia

The ABCs of Values to Live by...

Actions speak louder than words.

Be the cause of wonderful things.

Communicate compassionately.

Do what you can to help others.

Earn more than you spend.

Focus on the positive.

Give the world your best.

Have a sense of humor.

Improve your talents.

Just be true to yourself.

Know what you value.

Live each day to the fullest.

Make time to say "I love you."

Never give up on your dreams.

Own your attitude and behavior.

Practice what you preach.

Quest for a life of purpose.

Relish the little things in life.

Stand up for what you believe.

Transform intentions into deeds.

Understand more, judge less.

View difficulties as opportunities.

Work to realize your dreams.

Xercise your conscience.

Yearn to make a difference.

Zest to love and serve.

I expect to pass through this world but once; any good thing therefore that I can do, or any kindness that I can show to any fellow creature, let me do it now; let me not defer or neglect it, for I shall not pass this way again.

~Etienne de Grellet

Feed the hungry, heal the sick, then take a rest. Never walk when you can dance; make your home a cozy nest.

~Marshall B. Rosenberg

May you always have...

Wealth

enough to share

*T*he greatest gifts we can give to others are not material things but gifts of ourselves. The great gifts are those of love, of inspiration, of kindness, of encouragement, of forgiveness, of ideas and ideals.

~Author unknown

*T*he miracle is this—the more we share, the more we have.

~Leonard Nimoy

Do whatever comes your way to do as well as you can.
Think as little as possible about yourself and as much as
possible about other people....Put a good deal of thought into
the happiness that you are able to give.

~Eleanor Roosevelt

We make a living by what we get,
but we make a life by what we give.

~Henry Bucher

May you always have...Wealth enough to share

*Spread love everywhere you go;
first of all in your own house.*

~Mother Teresa

*I have found that there is a tremendous joy in giving.
It is a very important part of the joy of living.*

~William Black

Could I climb to the highest place in Athens,
I would lift my voice and proclaim,
"Fellow citizens, why do you turn and scrape every stone
to gather wealth and take so little care of your children
to whom one day you must relinquish it all?"

~Socrates

Our work-a-day lives are filled with opportunities to bless others. The power of a single glance or an encouraging smile must never be underestimated.

~G. Richard Rieger

The greatest good we can do for others is not to share our riches but to reveal theirs.

~Gil Atkinson

May you always have...

Xuberance

for your xistence

What a wonderful life I've had! I only wish I'd realized it sooner.

~Sidonie-Gabrielle Colette

*I want to learn to live each moment
and be grateful for what it brings, asking no more.*

~Gloria Gaither

*The most beautiful thing in the world is, of course,
the world itself.*

~Wallace Stevens

*In the name of God, stop a moment,
cease your work, look around you.*

~Leo Tolstoy

Exuberance is beauty.

~William Blake

*Oh, my friend, it's not what they take away from you that counts.
It's what you do with what you have left.*

~Hubert Humphrey

Thankfulness sets in motion a chain reaction that transforms people all around us, including ourselves. For no one ever misunderstands the melody of a grateful heart. Its message is universal; its lyrics transcend all earthly barriers; its music touches the heavens.

~Fred Bauer

Persons thankful for little things are certain to be the ones with much to be thankful for.

~Frank Clark

May you always have...

Youthfulness

of spirit

The secret of genius is to carry the spirit of the child into old age,
which means never losing your enthusiasm.

~Aldous Huxley

We do not stop playing because we are old.
We grow old because we stop playing.
The world is your playground. Why aren't you playing?

~Author unknown

You can't help getting older, but you don't have to get old.
New dreams, new works in progress—
that's the ticket for a long and happy ride.

~George Burns

Though we travel the world over to find the beautiful,
we must carry it with us or we find it not.

~Ralph Waldo Emerson

There's a natural method for recapturing youth....
The remedy requires no money, physician, nor magic.
Just go out in the field and begin to dig and plough.

~Johann Wolfgang von Goethe

The young do not know enough to be prudent,
and therefore they attempt the impossible—
and achieve it, generation after generation.

~Pearl S. Buck

May you always have...

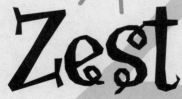

Zest

to make a difference

You really can change the world if you care enough.

~Marian Wright Edelman

Things you do for other people are usually the best things you do.

~Author unknown

If you can't feed a hundred people, then feed just one.

~Mother Teresa

I believe...that every human mind
feels pleasure in doing good to another.

~Thomas Jefferson

I don't know what your destiny will be, but one thing I know:
the only happy ones among you who will be truly happy
are those who will have sought and found a way to serve.

~Albert Schweitzer

Do what you can, with what you have, where you are.

~Theodore Roosevelt

*If your real desire is to do good,
there is no need to wait for money before you do it;
you can do it now, this very moment, and just where you are.*

~James Allen

Little ABC gift books, big messages

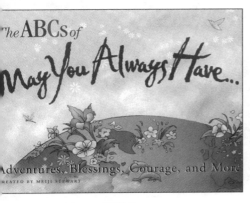

#1871

1872

Little gift books, big messages

#8313

Keep Coming Back

#6608

#6456

#6460

To order these great gift books, call 1-800-328-9000 or go to *www.hazelden.org/bookplace*

Little gift books, big messages

6458

6568

6569

Happiness is an **Inside** Job

Humor & wisdom
celebrating
the art of happiness

6566

Little gift books, big messages

#6457

#6570

#1737

#1736

To order these great gift books, call 1-800-328-9000 or go to *www.hazelden.org/bookplace*

HAZELDEN

Keep Coming Back™

Complimentary Catalog Available
Hazelden, P.O. Box 176, Center City, MN 55012-0176
1-800-328-9000   www.hazelden.org

Hazelden/Keep Coming Back titles available from your favorite bookstore:

The ABCs of Dare to...	ISBN 1-56838-744-X
The ABCs of May You Always Have...	ISBN 1-56838-745-8
Relax, God Is in Charge	ISBN 1-56838-377-0
Keep Coming Back	ISBN 1-56838-378-9
Children Are Meant to Be Seen and Heard	ISBN 1-56838-379-7
Shoot for the Moon	ISBN 1-56838-380-0
When Life Gives You Lemons…	ISBN 1-56838-381-9
It's a Jungle Out There!	ISBN 1-56838-382-7
Parenting...Part Joy...Part Guerrilla Warfare	ISBN 1-56838-383-5
God Danced the Day You Were Born	ISBN 1-56838-384-3
Happiness Is an Inside Job	ISBN 1-56838-385-1
Anything Is Possible	ISBN 1-56838-386-X
Follow Your Dreams	ISBN 1-56838-514-5
Friends	ISBN 1-56838-515-3

Acknowledgments

Every effort has been made to find the copyright owner of the material used. However, there are a few quotations that have been impossible to trace, and we would be glad to hear from the copyright owners of these quotations so that acknowledgment can be recognized in any future edition.